MW00896442

DEDICATION

FAMILY MOVIE JOURNAL
IS DEDICATED TO MY CHILDREN,
DREW AND CAYLEE AND MY HUSBAND
JEFF, WHO WILL FOREVER BE THE MOST
IMPORTANT CONNECTIONS I HAVE IN MY
LIFE. OF COURSE, I MUST INCLUDE OUR
SWEET LOVING RHODESIAN RIDGEBACK,
WHO MAKES EVERYTHING BETTER
WHEN SHE IS WITH US.

CONNECT • SHARE • ENJOY

FAMILY MOVIE Journal

LAURIE ARRON

© 2017 Laurie Arron

All Rights Reserved

MOVIE NAME

TODAY IS:

RATING

⭐ ⭐ ⭐ ⭐ ⭐

STARRING

What did you like or dislike

about the movie?

What did you learn

from the movie?

WATCH IT AGAIN?

YES
ONLY IF THERE
IS POPCORN
NO

RECOMMEND IT?

YES
UMMMM.....
NO

FAVORITE CHARACTER
and WHY?

FAVORITE QUOTE OR LINE

MOVIE GENRE

FAMILY FAVORITE?
YES ? NO

WHO SELECTED IT?

WHO IS WATCHING?

MOVIE NAME

TODAY IS:

RATING

★ ★ ★ ★ ★

STARRING

What did you like or dislike about the movie?

What did you learn from the movie?

FAVORITE CHARACTER and WHY?

MOVIE GENRE

FAMILY FAVORITE?

YES ? NO

WHO SELECTED IT?

WHO IS WATCHING?

FAVORITE QUOTE OR LINE

WATCH IT AGAIN?

YES
ONLY IF THERE IS POPCORN
NO

RECOMMEND IT?

YES
UMMMM.....
NO

MOVIE NAME

TODAY IS:

RATING

★ ★ ★ ★ ★

STARRING

What did you like or dislike about the movie?

What did you learn from the movie?

FAVORITE CHARACTER
and WHY?

FAVORITE QUOTE OR LINE

MOVIE GENRE

FAMILY FAVORITE?
YES   ?   NO

WHO SELECTED IT?

WHO IS WATCHING?

WATCH IT AGAIN?

YES
ONLY IF THERE IS POPCORN
NO

RECOMMEND IT?

YES
UMMMM.....
NO

MOVIE NAME

TODAY IS:

RATING

☆ ☆ ☆ ☆ ☆

STARRING

What did you like or dislike about the movie?

What did you learn from the movie?

FAVORITE CHARACTER and WHY?

MOVIE GENRE

FAMILY FAVORITE?
YES ? NO

WHO SELECTED IT?

WHO IS WATCHING?

FAVORITE QUOTE OR LINE

WATCH IT AGAIN?

YES

ONLY IF THERE IS POPCORN

NO

RECOMMEND IT?

YES

UMMMM.....

NO

MOVIE NAME

TODAY IS:

RATING

STARRING

What did you like or dislike about the movie?

What did you learn from the movie?

FAVORITE CHARACTER and WHY?

MOVIE GENRE

FAMILY FAVORITE?
YES ? NO

WHO SELECTED IT?

WHO IS WATCHING?

FAVORITE QUOTE OR LINE

WATCH IT AGAIN?

YES
ONLY IF THERE IS POPCORN
NO

RECOMMEND IT?

YES
UMMMM.....
NO

MOVIE NAME

TODAY IS:

RATING

☆ ☆ ☆ ☆ ☆

STARRING

What did you like or dislike

about the movie?

What did you learn

from the movie?

FAVORITE CHARACTER
and WHY?

MOVIE GENRE

FAMILY FAVORITE?

YES ? NO

WHO SELECTED IT?

WHO IS WATCHING?

FAVORITE QUOTE OR LINE

WATCH IT AGAIN?

YES

ONLY IF THERE
IS POPCORN

NO

RECOMMEND IT?

YES

UMMMM.....

NO

MOVIE NAME

TODAY IS:

RATING

★ ★ ★ ★ ★

STARRING

What did you like or dislike about the movie?

What did you learn from the movie?

FAVORITE CHARACTER and WHY?

MOVIE GENRE

FAMILY FAVORITE?
YES ? NO

WHO SELECTED IT?

WHO IS WATCHING?

FAVORITE QUOTE OR LINE

WATCH IT AGAIN?

YES
ONLY IF THERE IS POPCORN
NO

RECOMMEND IT?

YES
UMMMM.....
NO

MOVIE NAME

TODAY IS:

RATING

★ ★ ★ ★ ★

STARRING

What did you like or dislike about the movie?

What did you learn from the movie?

FAVORITE CHARACTER and WHY?

FAVORITE QUOTE OR LINE

MOVIE GENRE

FAMILY FAVORITE?
YES ? NO

WHO SELECTED IT?

WHO IS WATCHING?

WATCH IT AGAIN?

YES
ONLY IF THERE IS POPCORN
NO

RECOMMEND IT?

YES
UMMMM.....
NO

MOVIE NAME

TODAY IS:

RATING

★ ★ ★ ★ ★

STARRING

What did you like or dislike about the movie?

What did you learn from the movie?

WATCH IT AGAIN?

YES
ONLY IF THERE IS POPCORN
NO

RECOMMEND IT?

YES
UMMMM.....
NO

FAVORITE CHARACTER and WHY?

FAVORITE QUOTE OR LINE

MOVIE GENRE

FAMILY FAVORITE?
YES ? NO

WHO SELECTED IT?

WHO IS WATCHING?

MOVIE NAME

TODAY IS:

RATING

☆ ☆ ☆ ☆ ☆

STARRING

What did you like or dislike about the movie?

What did you learn from the movie?

FAVORITE CHARACTER and WHY?

MOVIE GENRE

FAMILY FAVORITE?
YES ? NO

WHO SELECTED IT?

WHO IS WATCHING?

FAVORITE QUOTE OR LINE

WATCH IT AGAIN?
YES
ONLY IF THERE IS POPCORN
NO

RECOMMEND IT?
YES
UMMMM.....
NO

MOVIE NAME

TODAY IS:

RATING

STARRING

What did you like or dislike about the movie?

What did you learn from the movie?

WATCH IT AGAIN?

YES

ONLY IF THERE IS POPCORN

NO

RECOMMEND IT?

YES

UMMMM.....

NO

FAVORITE CHARACTER and WHY?

MOVIE GENRE

FAMILY FAVORITE?

YES ? NO

WHO SELECTED IT?

WHO IS WATCHING?

FAVORITE QUOTE OR LINE

MOVIE NAME

TODAY IS:

RATING

☆ ☆ ☆ ☆ ☆

STARRING

What did you like or dislike about the movie?

What did you learn from the movie?

WATCH IT AGAIN?

YES
ONLY IF THERE IS POPCORN
NO

RECOMMEND IT?

YES
UMMMM.....
NO

FAVORITE CHARACTER
and WHY?

FAVORITE QUOTE OR LINE

MOVIE GENRE

FAMILY FAVORITE?
YES ? NO

WHO SELECTED IT?

WHO IS WATCHING?

MOVIE NAME

TODAY IS:

RATING

STARRING

What did you like or dislike about the movie?

What did you learn from the movie?

FAVORITE CHARACTER and WHY?

MOVIE GENRE

FAMILY FAVORITE?
YES ? NO

WHO SELECTED IT?

WHO IS WATCHING?

FAVORITE QUOTE OR LINE

WATCH IT AGAIN?

YES
ONLY IF THERE IS POPCORN
NO

RECOMMEND IT?

YES
UMMMM.....
NO

MOVIE NAME

TODAY IS:

RATING

☆ ☆ ☆ ☆ ☆

STARRING

What did you like or dislike about the movie?

What did you learn from the movie?

FAVORITE CHARACTER *and* WHY?

MOVIE GENRE

FAMILY FAVORITE?
YES ? NO

WHO SELECTED IT?

WHO IS WATCHING?

FAVORITE QUOTE OR LINE

WATCH IT AGAIN?

YES
ONLY IF THERE IS POPCORN
NO

RECOMMEND IT?

YES
UMMMM.....
NO

MOVIE NAME

TODAY IS:

RATING

★ ★ ★ ★ ★

STARRING

What did you like or dislike about the movie?

What did you learn from the movie?

FAVORITE CHARACTER and WHY?

MOVIE GENRE

FAMILY FAVORITE?
YES ? NO

WHO SELECTED IT?

WHO IS WATCHING?

FAVORITE QUOTE OR LINE

WATCH IT AGAIN?

YES
ONLY IF THERE IS POPCORN
NO

RECOMMEND IT?

YES
UMMMM.....
NO

MOVIE NAME

TODAY IS:

RATING

★ ★ ★ ★ ★

STARRING

What did you like or dislike about the movie?

from the movie?

What did you learn

FAVORITE CHARACTER and WHY?

MOVIE GENRE

FAMILY FAVORITE?

YES ? NO

WHO SELECTED IT?

WHO IS WATCHING?

FAVORITE QUOTE OR LINE

WATCH IT AGAIN?

YES
ONLY IF THERE IS POPCORN
NO

RECOMMEND IT?

YES
UMMMM.....
NO

MOVIE NAME

TODAY IS:

RATING

☆ ☆ ☆ ☆ ☆

STARRING

What did you like or dislike about the movie?

What did you learn from the movie?

FAVORITE CHARACTER and WHY?

MOVIE GENRE

FAMILY FAVORITE?
YES ? NO

WHO SELECTED IT?

WHO IS WATCHING?

FAVORITE QUOTE OR LINE

WATCH IT AGAIN?

YES
ONLY IF THERE IS POPCORN
NO

RECOMMEND IT?

YES
UMMMM.....
NO

MOVIE NAME

TODAY IS:

RATING

★ ★ ★ ★ ★

STARRING

What did you like or dislike about the movie?

What did you learn from the movie?

WATCH IT AGAIN?

YES
ONLY IF THERE
IS POPCORN
NO

RECOMMEND IT?

YES
UMMMM......
NO

FAVORITE CHARACTER *and* WHY?

FAVORITE QUOTE OR LINE

MOVIE GENRE

FAMILY FAVORITE?
YES ? NO

WHO SELECTED IT?

WHO IS WATCHING?

MOVIE NAME

TODAY IS:

RATING

STARRING

What did you like or dislike about the movie?

What did you learn from the movie?

FAVORITE CHARACTER and WHY?

MOVIE GENRE

FAMILY FAVORITE?
YES ? NO

WHO SELECTED IT?

WHO IS WATCHING?

FAVORITE QUOTE OR LINE

WATCH IT AGAIN?

YES
ONLY IF THERE IS POPCORN
NO

RECOMMEND IT?

YES
UMMMM.....
NO

MOVIE NAME

TODAY IS:

RATING

★ ★ ★ ★ ★

STARRING

What did you like or dislike about the movie?

FAVORITE CHARACTER and WHY?

MOVIE GENRE

FAMILY FAVORITE?
YES ? NO

WHO SELECTED IT?

What did you learn from the movie?

WHO IS WATCHING?

FAVORITE QUOTE OR LINE

WATCH IT AGAIN?

YES
ONLY IF THERE IS POPCORN
NO

RECOMMEND IT?

YES
UMMMM.....
NO

MOVIE NAME

TODAY IS:

RATING

STARRING

What did you like or dislike about the movie?

What did you learn from the movie?

FAVORITE CHARACTER *and* WHY?

MOVIE GENRE

FAMILY FAVORITE?
YES ? NO

WHO SELECTED IT?

WHO IS WATCHING?

FAVORITE QUOTE OR LINE

WATCH IT AGAIN?

YES
ONLY IF THERE IS POPCORN
NO

RECOMMEND IT?

YES
UMMMM.....
NO

MOVIE NAME

TODAY IS:

RATING

★ ★ ★ ★ ★

STARRING

What did you like or dislike about the movie?

What did you learn from the movie?

FAVORITE CHARACTER and WHY?

MOVIE GENRE

FAMILY FAVORITE?
YES ? NO

WHO SELECTED IT?

WHO IS WATCHING?

FAVORITE QUOTE OR LINE

WATCH IT AGAIN?

YES
ONLY IF THERE IS POPCORN
NO

RECOMMEND IT?

YES
UMMMM.....
NO

MOVIE NAME

TODAY IS:

RATING

⭐ ⭐ ⭐ ⭐ ⭐

STARRING

What did you like or dislike about the movie?

What did you learn from the movie?

FAVORITE CHARACTER *and* WHY?

MOVIE GENRE

FAMILY FAVORITE?
YES ? NO

WHO SELECTED IT?

WHO IS WATCHING?

FAVORITE QUOTE OR LINE

WATCH IT AGAIN?

YES
ONLY IF THERE IS POPCORN
NO

RECOMMEND IT?

YES
UMMMM.....
NO

MOVIE NAME

TODAY IS:

RATING

★ ★ ★ ★ ★

STARRING

What did you like or dislike about the movie?

What did you learn from the movie?

WATCH IT AGAIN?

YES
ONLY IF THERE IS POPCORN
NO

RECOMMEND IT?

YES
UMMMM.....
NO

FAVORITE CHARACTER *and* WHY?

MOVIE GENRE

FAMILY FAVORITE?
YES ? NO

WHO SELECTED IT?

WHO IS WATCHING?

FAVORITE QUOTE OR LINE

MOVIE NAME

TODAY IS:

RATING

★ ★ ★ ★ ★

STARRING

What did you like or dislike about the movie?

from the movie?

What did you learn

FAVORITE CHARACTER and WHY?

FAVORITE QUOTE OR LINE

MOVIE GENRE

FAMILY FAVORITE?

YES ? NO

WHO SELECTED IT?

WHO IS WATCHING?

WATCH IT AGAIN?

YES
ONLY IF THERE IS POPCORN
NO

RECOMMEND IT?

YES
UMMMM.....
NO

MOVIE NAME

TODAY IS:

RATING

★ ★ ★ ★ ★

STARRING

What did you like or dislike about the movie?

What did you learn from the movie?

FAVORITE CHARACTER *and* WHY?

MOVIE GENRE

FAMILY FAVORITE?

YES ? NO

WHO SELECTED IT?

WHO IS WATCHING?

FAVORITE QUOTE OR LINE

WATCH IT AGAIN?

YES
ONLY IF THERE IS POPCORN
NO

RECOMMEND IT?

YES
UMMMM.....
NO

MOVIE NAME

TODAY IS:

RATING

★ ★ ★ ★ ★

STARRING

What did you like or dislike about the movie?

What did you learn from the movie?

FAVORITE CHARACTER and WHY?

MOVIE GENRE

FAMILY FAVORITE?
YES ? NO

WHO SELECTED IT?

WHO IS WATCHING?

FAVORITE QUOTE OR LINE

WATCH IT AGAIN?

YES
ONLY IF THERE IS POPCORN
NO

RECOMMEND IT?

YES
UMMMM.....
NO

MOVIE NAME

TODAY IS:

RATING

☆ ☆ ☆ ☆ ☆

STARRING

What did you like or dislike about the movie?

What did you learn from the movie?

FAVORITE CHARACTER and WHY?

MOVIE GENRE

FAMILY FAVORITE?
YES ? NO

WHO SELECTED IT?

WHO IS WATCHING?

FAVORITE QUOTE OR LINE

WATCH IT AGAIN?

YES
ONLY IF THERE IS POPCORN
NO

RECOMMEND IT?
YES
UMMMM.....
NO

MOVIE NAME

TODAY IS:

RATING

STARRING

What did you like or dislike about the movie?

What did you learn from the movie?

FAVORITE CHARACTER and WHY?

MOVIE GENRE

FAMILY FAVORITE?
YES ? NO

WHO SELECTED IT?

WHO IS WATCHING?

FAVORITE QUOTE OR LINE

WATCH IT AGAIN?

YES
ONLY IF THERE IS POPCORN
NO

RECOMMEND IT?

YES
UMMMM.....
NO

MOVIE NAME

TODAY IS:

RATING

★ ★ ★ ★ ★

STARRING

What did you like or dislike about the movie?

What did you learn from the movie?

FAVORITE CHARACTER and WHY?

MOVIE GENRE

FAMILY FAVORITE?
YES ? NO

WHO SELECTED IT?

WHO IS WATCHING?

FAVORITE QUOTE OR LINE

WATCH IT AGAIN?
YES
ONLY IF THERE IS POPCORN
NO

RECOMMEND IT?
YES
UMMMM.....
NO

MOVIE NAME

TODAY IS:

RATING

STARRING

What did you like or dislike about the movie?

What did you learn from the movie?

FAVORITE CHARACTER and WHY?

MOVIE GENRE

FAMILY FAVORITE?
YES ? NO

WHO SELECTED IT?

WHO IS WATCHING?

FAVORITE QUOTE OR LINE

WATCH IT AGAIN?

YES
ONLY IF THERE IS POPCORN
NO

RECOMMEND IT?

YES
UMMMM.....
NO

MOVIE NAME

TODAY IS:

RATING

★ ★ ★ ★ ★

STARRING

What did you like or dislike about the movie?

What did you learn from the movie?

FAVORITE CHARACTER and WHY?

MOVIE GENRE

FAMILY FAVORITE?
YES ? NO

WHO SELECTED IT?

WHO IS WATCHING?

FAVORITE QUOTE OR LINE

WATCH IT AGAIN?

YES
ONLY IF THERE IS POPCORN
NO

RECOMMEND IT?

YES
UMMMM.....
NO

MOVIE NAME

TODAY IS:

RATING

★ ★ ★ ★ ★

STARRING

What did you like or dislike about the movie?

What did you learn from the movie?

WATCH IT AGAIN?

YES
ONLY IF THERE IS POPCORN
NO

RECOMMEND IT?

YES
UMMMM.....
NO

FAVORITE CHARACTER and WHY?

FAVORITE QUOTE OR LINE

MOVIE GENRE

FAMILY FAVORITE?
YES ? NO

WHO SELECTED IT?

WHO IS WATCHING?

MOVIE NAME

TODAY IS:

RATING

★ ★ ★ ★ ★

STARRING

What did you like or dislike about the movie?

What did you learn from the movie?

WATCH IT AGAIN?

YES

ONLY IF THERE IS POPCORN

NO

RECOMMEND IT?

YES

UMMMM.....

NO

FAVORITE CHARACTER and WHY?

MOVIE GENRE

FAMILY FAVORITE?

YES ? NO

WHO SELECTED IT?

WHO IS WATCHING?

FAVORITE QUOTE OR LINE

MOVIE NAME

TODAY IS:

RATING

STARRING

What did you like or dislike about the movie?

What did you learn from the movie?

FAVORITE CHARACTER and WHY?

MOVIE GENRE

FAMILY FAVORITE?
YES ? NO

WHO SELECTED IT?

WHO IS WATCHING?

FAVORITE QUOTE OR LINE

WATCH IT AGAIN?

YES
ONLY IF THERE IS POPCORN
NO

RECOMMEND IT?

YES
UMMMM.....
NO

MOVIE NAME

TODAY IS:

RATING

STARRING

What did you like or dislike about the movie?

FAVORITE CHARACTER and WHY?

MOVIE GENRE

FAMILY FAVORITE?
YES ? NO

WHO SELECTED IT?

What did you learn from the movie?

WHO IS WATCHING?

FAVORITE QUOTE OR LINE

WATCH IT AGAIN?

YES
ONLY IF THERE IS POPCORN
NO

RECOMMEND IT?

YES
UMMMM.....
NO

MOVIE NAME

TODAY IS:

RATING

⭐ ⭐ ⭐ ⭐ ⭐

STARRING

What did you like or dislike about the movie?

What did you learn from the movie?

WATCH IT AGAIN?

YES
ONLY IF THERE IS POPCORN
NO

RECOMMEND IT?

YES
UMMMM.....
NO

FAVORITE CHARACTER and WHY?

FAVORITE QUOTE OR LINE

MOVIE GENRE

FAMILY FAVORITE?
YES ? NO

WHO SELECTED IT?

WHO IS WATCHING?

MOVIE NAME

TODAY IS:

RATING

☆ ☆ ☆ ☆ ☆

STARRING

What did you like or dislike about the movie?

What did you learn from the movie?

WATCH IT AGAIN?

YES
ONLY IF THERE
IS POPCORN
NO

RECOMMEND IT?

YES
UMMMM.....
NO

FAVORITE CHARACTER *and* WHY?

FAVORITE QUOTE OR LINE

MOVIE GENRE

FAMILY FAVORITE?
YES ? NO

WHO SELECTED IT?

WHO IS WATCHING?

TODAY IS:

MOVIE NAME

RATING
⭐ ⭐ ⭐ ⭐ ⭐

STARRING

What did you like or dislike about the movie?

What did you learn from the movie?

FAVORITE CHARACTER and WHY?

MOVIE GENRE

FAMILY FAVORITE?
YES ? NO

WHO SELECTED IT?

WHO IS WATCHING?

FAVORITE QUOTE OR LINE

WATCH IT AGAIN?

YES
ONLY IF THERE IS POPCORN
NO

RECOMMEND IT?

YES
UMMMM.....
NO

MOVIE NAME

TODAY IS:

RATING

STARRING

What did you like or dislike about the movie?

FAVORITE CHARACTER and WHY?

MOVIE GENRE

FAMILY FAVORITE?

YES ? NO

WHO SELECTED IT?

What did you learn from the movie?

WHO IS WATCHING?

FAVORITE QUOTE OR LINE

WATCH IT AGAIN?

YES
ONLY IF THERE IS POPCORN
NO

RECOMMEND IT?

YES
UMMMM.....
NO

MOVIE NAME

TODAY IS:

RATING

★ ★ ★ ★ ★

STARRING

What did you like or dislike

about the movie?

from the movie?

What did you learn

FAVORITE CHARACTER
and WHY?

MOVIE GENRE

FAMILY FAVORITE?
YES ? NO

WHO SELECTED IT?

WHO IS WATCHING?

FAVORITE QUOTE OR LINE

WATCH IT AGAIN?

YES
ONLY IF THERE
IS POPCORN
NO

RECOMMEND IT?

YES
UMMMM.....
NO

MOVIE NAME

TODAY IS:

RATING

★ ★ ★ ★ ★

STARRING

What did you like or dislike about the movie?

What did you learn from the movie?

WATCH IT AGAIN?

YES

ONLY IF THERE IS POPCORN

NO

RECOMMEND IT?

YES

UMMMM.....

NO

FAVORITE CHARACTER and WHY?

FAVORITE QUOTE OR LINE

MOVIE GENRE

FAMILY FAVORITE?

YES ? NO

WHO SELECTED IT?

WHO IS WATCHING?

MOVIE NAME

TODAY IS:

RATING

STARRING

What did you like or dislike about the movie?

What did you learn from the movie?

FAVORITE CHARACTER and WHY?

MOVIE GENRE

FAMILY FAVORITE?
YES ? NO

WHO SELECTED IT?

WHO IS WATCHING?

FAVORITE QUOTE OR LINE

WATCH IT AGAIN?

YES
ONLY IF THERE
IS POPCORN
NO

RECOMMEND IT?

YES
UMMMM.....
NO

MOVIE NAME

TODAY IS:

RATING

☆ ☆ ☆ ☆ ☆

STARRING

What did you like or dislike about the movie?

What did you learn from the movie?

FAVORITE CHARACTER *and,* WHY?

FAVORITE QUOTE OR LINE

MOVIE GENRE

FAMILY FAVORITE?
YES ? NO

WHO SELECTED IT?

WHO IS WATCHING?

WATCH IT AGAIN?
YES
ONLY IF THERE IS POPCORN
NO

RECOMMEND IT?
YES
UMMMM.....
NO

MOVIE NAME

TODAY IS:

RATING

★ ★ ★ ★ ★

STARRING

What did you like or dislike about the movie?

What did you learn from the movie?

WATCH IT AGAIN?

YES
ONLY IF THERE IS POPCORN
NO

RECOMMEND IT?

YES
UMMMM.....
NO

FAVORITE CHARACTER and WHY?

MOVIE GENRE

FAMILY FAVORITE?
YES ? NO

WHO SELECTED IT?

WHO IS WATCHING?

FAVORITE QUOTE OR LINE

MOVIE NAME

TODAY IS:

RATING

★ ★ ★ ★ ★

STARRING

What did you like or dislike about the movie?

What did you learn from the movie?

WATCH IT AGAIN?

YES
ONLY IF THERE IS POPCORN
NO

RECOMMEND IT?

YES
UMMMM.....
NO

FAVORITE CHARACTER and WHY?

FAVORITE QUOTE OR LINE

MOVIE GENRE

FAMILY FAVORITE?
YES ? NO

WHO SELECTED IT?

WHO IS WATCHING?

MOVIE NAME

TODAY IS:

RATING

☆ ☆ ☆ ☆ ☆

STARRING

What did you like or dislike about the movie?

What did you learn from the movie?

WATCH IT AGAIN?

YES
ONLY IF THERE
IS POPCORN
NO

RECOMMEND IT?

YES
UMMMM.....
NO

FAVORITE CHARACTER *and* WHY?

FAVORITE QUOTE OR LINE

MOVIE GENRE

FAMILY FAVORITE?
YES ? NO

WHO SELECTED IT?

WHO IS WATCHING?

MOVIE NAME

TODAY IS:

RATING

★ ★ ★ ★ ★

What did you like or dislike about the movie?

What did you learn from the movie?

WATCH IT AGAIN?

YES
ONLY IF THERE IS POPCORN
NO

RECOMMEND IT?

YES
UMMMM.....
NO

STARRING

FAVORITE CHARACTER and WHY?

FAVORITE QUOTE OR LINE

MOVIE GENRE

FAMILY FAVORITE?
YES ? NO

WHO SELECTED IT?

WHO IS WATCHING?

MOVIE NAME

TODAY IS:

RATING

⭐ ⭐ ⭐ ⭐ ⭐

STARRING

What did you like or dislike

about the movie?

from the movie?

What did you learn

FAVORITE CHARACTER and WHY?

FAVORITE QUOTE OR LINE

MOVIE GENRE

FAMILY FAVORITE?

YES ? NO

WHO SELECTED IT?

WHO IS WATCHING?

WATCH IT AGAIN?

YES

ONLY IF THERE IS POPCORN

NO

RECOMMEND IT?

YES

UMMMM.....

NO

MOVIE NAME

TODAY IS:

RATING

☆ ☆ ☆ ☆ ☆

STARRING

What did you like or dislike about the movie?

What did you learn from the movie?

WATCH IT AGAIN?

YES
ONLY IF THERE IS POPCORN
NO

RECOMMEND IT?

YES
UMMMM.....
NO

FAVORITE CHARACTER
and WHY?

FAVORITE QUOTE OR LINE

MOVIE GENRE

FAMILY FAVORITE?
YES ? NO

WHO SELECTED IT?

WHO IS WATCHING?

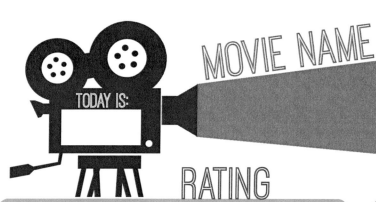

MOVIE NAME

TODAY IS:

RATING

STARRING

What did you like or dislike about the movie?

What did you learn from the movie?

WATCH IT AGAIN?

YES
ONLY IF THERE IS POPCORN
NO

RECOMMEND IT?

YES
UMMMM......
NO

FAVORITE CHARACTER and WHY?

MOVIE GENRE

FAMILY FAVORITE?

YES ? NO

WHO SELECTED IT?

WHO IS WATCHING?

FAVORITE QUOTE OR LINE

MOVIE NAME

TODAY IS:

RATING

⭐ ⭐ ⭐ ⭐ ⭐

STARRING

What did you like or dislike

about the movie?

What did you learn

from the movie?

FAVORITE CHARACTER and WHY?

MOVIE GENRE

FAMILY FAVORITE?

YES ? NO

WHO SELECTED IT?

WHO IS WATCHING?

FAVORITE QUOTE OR LINE

WATCH IT AGAIN?

YES

ONLY IF THERE IS POPCORN

NO

RECOMMEND IT?

YES

UMMMM.....

NO

MOVIE NAME

TODAY IS:

RATING

STARRING

What did you like or dislike about the movie?

What did you learn from the movie?

FAVORITE CHARACTER and, WHY?

MOVIE GENRE

FAMILY FAVORITE?

YES ? NO

WHO SELECTED IT?

WHO IS WATCHING?

FAVORITE QUOTE OR LINE

WATCH IT AGAIN?

YES

ONLY IF THERE IS POPCORN

NO

RECOMMEND IT?

YES

UMMMM.....

NO

MOVIE NAME

TODAY IS:

RATING

★ ★ ★ ★ ★

STARRING

What did you like or dislike about the movie?

What did you learn from the movie?

WATCH IT AGAIN?

YES
ONLY IF THERE
IS POPCORN
NO

RECOMMEND IT?

YES
UMMMM.....
NO

FAVORITE CHARACTER
and WHY?

MOVIE GENRE

FAMILY FAVORITE?
YES ? NO

WHO SELECTED IT?

WHO IS WATCHING?

FAVORITE QUOTE OR LINE

MOVIE NAME

TODAY IS:

RATING

STARRING

What did you like or dislike about the movie?

FAVORITE CHARACTER and WHY?

MOVIE GENRE

FAMILY FAVORITE?
YES ? NO

WHO SELECTED IT?

What did you learn from the movie?

WHO IS WATCHING?

FAVORITE QUOTE OR LINE

WATCH IT AGAIN?

YES
ONLY IF THERE IS POPCORN
NO

RECOMMEND IT?

YES
UMMMM.....
NO

MOVIE NAME

TODAY IS:

RATING

⭐ ⭐ ⭐ ⭐ ⭐

STARRING

What did you like or dislike about the movie?

What did you learn from the movie?

FAVORITE CHARACTER *and* WHY?

MOVIE GENRE

FAMILY FAVORITE?
YES ? NO

WHO SELECTED IT?

WHO IS WATCHING?

FAVORITE QUOTE OR LINE

WATCH IT AGAIN?

YES
ONLY IF THERE IS POPCORN
NO

RECOMMEND IT?

YES
UMMMM.....
NO

MOVIE NAME

TODAY IS:

RATING

STARRING

What did you like or dislike about the movie?

What did you learn from the movie?

FAVORITE CHARACTER and WHY?

MOVIE GENRE

FAMILY FAVORITE?
YES ? NO

WHO SELECTED IT?

WHO IS WATCHING?

FAVORITE QUOTE OR LINE

WATCH IT AGAIN?

RECOMMEND IT?

YES
ONLY IF THERE IS POPCORN
NO

YES
UMMMM.....
NO

MOVIE NAME

TODAY IS:

RATING

★ ★ ★ ★ ★

STARRING

What did you like or dislike about the movie?

What did you learn from the movie?

WATCH IT AGAIN?

YES
ONLY IF THERE IS POPCORN
NO

RECOMMEND IT?

YES
UMMMM.....
NO

FAVORITE CHARACTER and WHY?

FAVORITE QUOTE OR LINE

MOVIE GENRE

FAMILY FAVORITE?
YES ? NO

WHO SELECTED IT?

WHO IS WATCHING?

MOVIE NAME

TODAY IS:

RATING

STARRING

What did you like or dislike
about the movie?

What did you learn from the movie?

FAVORITE CHARACTER *and* WHY?

MOVIE GENRE

FAMILY FAVORITE?
YES ? NO

WHO SELECTED IT?

WHO IS WATCHING?

FAVORITE QUOTE OR LINE

WATCH IT AGAIN?
YES
ONLY IF THERE
IS POPCORN
NO

RECOMMEND IT?
YES
UMMMM.....
NO

MOVIE NAME

TODAY IS:

RATING

⭐ ⭐ ⭐ ⭐ ⭐

STARRING

What did you like or dislike about the movie?

FAVORITE CHARACTER and WHY?

MOVIE GENRE

FAMILY FAVORITE?
YES ? NO

WHO SELECTED IT?

What did you learn from the movie?

WHO IS WATCHING?

FAVORITE QUOTE OR LINE

WATCH IT AGAIN?
YES
ONLY IF THERE IS POPCORN
NO

RECOMMEND IT?
YES
UMMMM.....
NO

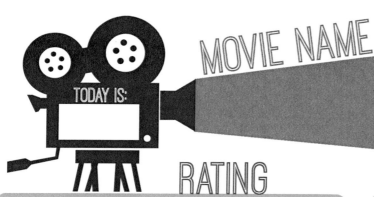

MOVIE NAME

TODAY IS:

RATING

☆ ☆ ☆ ☆ ☆

STARRING

What did you like or dislike about the movie?

What did you learn from the movie?

WATCH IT AGAIN?

YES
ONLY IF THERE IS POPCORN
NO

RECOMMEND IT?

YES
UMMMM.....
NO

FAVORITE CHARACTER and WHY?

MOVIE GENRE

FAMILY FAVORITE?
YES ? NO

WHO SELECTED IT?

WHO IS WATCHING?

FAVORITE QUOTE OR LINE

MOVIE NAME

TODAY IS:

RATING

⭐ ⭐ ⭐ ⭐ ⭐

STARRING

What did you like or dislike about the movie?

What did you learn from the movie?

FAVORITE CHARACTER and WHY?

FAVORITE QUOTE OR LINE

MOVIE GENRE

FAMILY FAVORITE?
YES ? NO

WHO SELECTED IT?

WHO IS WATCHING?

WATCH IT AGAIN?
YES
ONLY IF THERE IS POPCORN
NO

RECOMMEND IT?
YES
UMMMM.....
NO

MOVIE NAME

TODAY IS:

RATING

★ ★ ★ ★ ★

STARRING

What did you like or dislike about the movie?

What did you learn from the movie?

WATCH IT AGAIN?

YES
ONLY IF THERE IS POPCORN
NO

RECOMMEND IT?

YES
UMMMM.....
NO

FAVORITE CHARACTER and WHY?

FAVORITE QUOTE OR LINE

MOVIE GENRE

FAMILY FAVORITE?
YES ? NO

WHO SELECTED IT?

WHO IS WATCHING?

MOVIE NAME

TODAY IS:

RATING

⭐ ⭐ ⭐ ⭐ ⭐

STARRING

What did you like or dislike about the movie?

What did you learn from the movie?

FAVORITE CHARACTER *and* WHY?

MOVIE GENRE

FAMILY FAVORITE?
YES ? NO

WHO SELECTED IT?

WHO IS WATCHING?

FAVORITE QUOTE OR LINE

WATCH IT AGAIN?

YES
ONLY IF THERE IS POPCORN
NO

RECOMMEND IT?

YES
UMMMM.....
NO

TODAY IS:

MOVIE NAME

RATING

STARRING

What did you like or dislike about the movie?

What did you learn from the movie?

FAVORITE CHARACTER and, WHY?

MOVIE GENRE

FAMILY FAVORITE?
YES ? NO

WHO SELECTED IT?

WHO IS WATCHING?

FAVORITE QUOTE OR LINE

WATCH IT AGAIN?

YES
ONLY IF THERE IS POPCORN
NO

RECOMMEND IT?

YES
UMMMM.....
NO

MOVIE NAME

TODAY IS:

RATING

☆ ☆ ☆ ☆ ☆

STARRING

What did you like or dislike about the movie?

What did you learn from the movie?

WATCH IT AGAIN?

YES
ONLY IF THERE IS POPCORN
NO

RECOMMEND IT?

YES
UMMMM.....
NO

FAVORITE CHARACTER and WHY?

FAVORITE QUOTE OR LINE

MOVIE GENRE

FAMILY FAVORITE?
YES ? NO

WHO SELECTED IT?

WHO IS WATCHING?

MOVIE NAME

TODAY IS:

RATING

★ ★ ★ ★ ★

STARRING

What did you like or dislike about the movie?

FAVORITE CHARACTER *and* WHY?

MOVIE GENRE

FAMILY FAVORITE?

YES ? NO

WHO SELECTED IT?

What did you learn from the movie?

WHO IS WATCHING?

FAVORITE QUOTE OR LINE

WATCH IT AGAIN?

YES

ONLY IF THERE IS POPCORN

NO

RECOMMEND IT?

YES

UMMMM.....

NO

MOVIE NAME

TODAY IS:

RATING

☆ ☆ ☆ ☆ ☆

STARRING

What did you like or dislike about the movie?

What did you learn from the movie?

FAVORITE CHARACTER and WHY?

MOVIE GENRE

FAMILY FAVORITE?
YES ? NO

WHO SELECTED IT?

WHO IS WATCHING?

FAVORITE QUOTE OR LINE

WATCH IT AGAIN?
YES
ONLY IF THERE IS POPCORN
NO

RECOMMEND IT?
YES
UMMMM.....
NO

MOVIE NAME

TODAY IS:

RATING

STARRING

What did you like or dislike about the movie?

What did you learn from the movie?

FAVORITE CHARACTER and WHY?

MOVIE GENRE

FAMILY FAVORITE?

YES ? NO

WHO SELECTED IT?

WHO IS WATCHING?

FAVORITE QUOTE OR LINE

WATCH IT AGAIN?

YES
ONLY IF THERE IS POPCORN
NO

RECOMMEND IT?

YES
UMMMM.....
NO

MOVIE NAME

TODAY IS:

RATING

☆ ☆ ☆ ☆ ☆

STARRING

What did you like or dislike about the movie?

What did you learn from the movie?

FAVORITE CHARACTER and WHY?

MOVIE GENRE

FAMILY FAVORITE?
YES ? NO

WHO SELECTED IT?

WHO IS WATCHING?

FAVORITE QUOTE OR LINE

WATCH IT AGAIN?

YES
ONLY IF THERE IS POPCORN
NO

RECOMMEND IT?

YES
UMMMM.....
NO

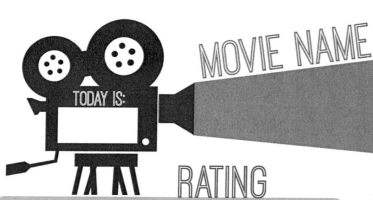

MOVIE NAME

TODAY IS:

RATING

☆ ☆ ☆ ☆ ☆

STARRING

What did you like or dislike about the movie?

What did you learn from the movie?

FAVORITE CHARACTER and WHY?

MOVIE GENRE

FAMILY FAVORITE?

YES ? NO

WHO SELECTED IT?

WHO IS WATCHING?

FAVORITE QUOTE OR LINE

WATCH IT AGAIN?

YES
ONLY IF THERE
IS POPCORN
NO

RECOMMEND IT?

YES
UMMMM.....
NO

MOVIE NAME

TODAY IS:

RATING

★ ★ ★ ★ ★

STARRING

What did you like or dislike about the movie?

What did you learn from the movie?

FAVORITE CHARACTER and WHY?

FAVORITE QUOTE OR LINE

MOVIE GENRE

FAMILY FAVORITE?
YES ? NO

WHO SELECTED IT?

WHO IS WATCHING?

WATCH IT AGAIN?

YES
ONLY IF THERE IS POPCORN
NO

RECOMMEND IT?

YES
UMMMM.....
NO

MOVIE NAME

TODAY IS:

RATING

★ ★ ★ ★ ★

STARRING

What did you like or dislike about the movie?

What did you learn from the movie?

FAVORITE CHARACTER and WHY?

MOVIE GENRE

FAMILY FAVORITE?
YES ? NO

WHO SELECTED IT?

WHO IS WATCHING?

FAVORITE QUOTE OR LINE

WATCH IT AGAIN?

YES
ONLY IF THERE IS POPCORN
NO

RECOMMEND IT?

YES
UMMMM.....
NO

MOVIE NAME

TODAY IS:

RATING

★ ★ ★ ★ ★

STARRING

What did you like or dislike about the movie?

FAVORITE CHARACTER and WHY?

MOVIE GENRE

FAMILY FAVORITE?
YES ? NO

What did you learn from the movie?

WHO SELECTED IT?

WHO IS WATCHING?

FAVORITE QUOTE OR LINE

WATCH IT AGAIN?

YES
ONLY IF THERE IS POPCORN
NO

RECOMMEND IT?

YES
UMMMM.....
NO

MOVIE NAME

TODAY IS:

RATING

STARRING

What did you like or dislike
about the movie?

FAVORITE CHARACTER *and* WHY?

MOVIE GENRE

FAMILY FAVORITE?
YES ? NO

WHO SELECTED IT?

What did you learn from the movie?

WHO IS WATCHING?

FAVORITE QUOTE OR LINE

WATCH IT AGAIN?

YES
ONLY IF THERE IS POPCORN
NO

RECOMMEND IT?

YES
UMMMM.....
NO

MOVIE NAME

TODAY IS:

RATING

★ ★ ★ ★ ★

STARRING

What did you like or dislike about the movie?

What did you learn from the movie?

FAVORITE CHARACTER and WHY?

MOVIE GENRE

FAMILY FAVORITE?
YES ? NO

WHO SELECTED IT?

WHO IS WATCHING?

FAVORITE QUOTE OR LINE

WATCH IT AGAIN?

YES
ONLY IF THERE IS POPCORN
NO

RECOMMEND IT?

YES
UMMMM.....
NO

MOVIE NAME

TODAY IS:

RATING

STARRING

What did you like or dislike about the movie?

What did you learn from the movie?

FAVORITE CHARACTER and WHY?

MOVIE GENRE

FAMILY FAVORITE?

YES ? NO

WHO SELECTED IT?

WHO IS WATCHING?

FAVORITE QUOTE OR LINE

WATCH IT AGAIN?

YES
ONLY IF THERE IS POPCORN
NO

RECOMMEND IT?

YES
UMMMM.....
NO

MOVIE NAME

TODAY IS:

RATING

★ ★ ★ ★ ★

STARRING

What did you like or dislike about the movie?

What did you learn from the movie?

WATCH IT AGAIN?

YES

ONLY IF THERE IS POPCORN

NO

RECOMMEND IT?

YES

UMMMM.....

NO

FAVORITE CHARACTER and WHY?

FAVORITE QUOTE OR LINE

MOVIE GENRE

FAMILY FAVORITE?

YES ? NO

WHO SELECTED IT?

WHO IS WATCHING?

MOVIE NAME

TODAY IS:

RATING

STARRING

What did you like or dislike about the movie?

What did you learn from the movie?

FAVORITE CHARACTER and WHY?

MOVIE GENRE

FAMILY FAVORITE?

YES ? NO

WHO SELECTED IT?

WHO IS WATCHING?

FAVORITE QUOTE OR LINE

WATCH IT AGAIN?

YES
ONLY IF THERE IS POPCORN
NO

RECOMMEND IT?

YES
UMMMM.....
NO

MOVIE NAME

TODAY IS:

RATING

⭐ ⭐ ⭐ ⭐ ⭐

STARRING

What did you like or dislike about the movie?

What did you learn from the movie?

FAVORITE CHARACTER and WHY?

FAVORITE QUOTE OR LINE

MOVIE GENRE

FAMILY FAVORITE?

YES ? NO

WHO SELECTED IT?

WHO IS WATCHING?

WATCH IT AGAIN?

YES
ONLY IF THERE IS POPCORN
NO

RECOMMEND IT?

YES
UMMMM.....
NO

MOVIE NAME

TODAY IS:

RATING

STARRING

What did you like or dislike about the movie?

What did you learn from the movie?

FAVORITE CHARACTER and WHY?

MOVIE GENRE

FAMILY FAVORITE?
YES ? NO

WHO SELECTED IT?

WHO IS WATCHING?

FAVORITE QUOTE OR LINE

WATCH IT AGAIN?

YES
ONLY IF THERE IS POPCORN
NO

RECOMMEND IT?

YES
UMMMM.....
NO

MOVIE NAME

TODAY IS:

RATING

STARRING

What did you like or dislike about the movie?

What did you learn from the movie?

FAVORITE CHARACTER
and WHY?

MOVIE GENRE

FAMILY FAVORITE?
YES ? NO

WHO SELECTED IT?

WHO IS WATCHING?

FAVORITE QUOTE OR LINE

WATCH IT AGAIN?

YES
ONLY IF THERE IS POPCORN
NO

RECOMMEND IT?

YES
UMMMM.....
NO

TODAY IS:

MOVIE NAME

RATING

STARRING

What did you like or dislike about the movie?

What did you learn from the movie?

FAVORITE CHARACTER *and,* WHY?

MOVIE GENRE

FAMILY FAVORITE?
YES ? NO

WHO SELECTED IT?

WHO IS WATCHING?

FAVORITE QUOTE OR LINE

WATCH IT AGAIN?
YES
ONLY IF THERE IS POPCORN
NO

RECOMMEND IT?
YES
UMMMM.....
NO

MOVIE NAME

TODAY IS:

RATING

☆ ☆ ☆ ☆ ☆

STARRING

What did you like or dislike about the movie?

What did you learn from the movie?

FAVORITE CHARACTER *and* WHY?

MOVIE GENRE

FAMILY FAVORITE?
YES ? NO

WHO SELECTED IT?

WHO IS WATCHING?

FAVORITE QUOTE OR LINE

WATCH IT AGAIN?
YES
ONLY IF THERE IS POPCORN
NO

RECOMMEND IT?
YES
UMMMM.....
NO

MOVIE NAME

TODAY IS:

RATING

☆ ☆ ☆ ☆ ☆

STARRING

What did you like or dislike about the movie?

from the movie?

What did you learn

FAVORITE CHARACTER and WHY?

MOVIE GENRE

FAMILY FAVORITE?
YES ? NO

WHO SELECTED IT?

WHO IS WATCHING?

FAVORITE QUOTE OR LINE

WATCH IT AGAIN?

YES
ONLY IF THERE IS POPCORN
NO

RECOMMEND IT?

YES
UMMMM.....
NO

MOVIE NAME

TODAY IS:

RATING

STARRING

What did you like or dislike about the movie?

What did you learn from the movie?

WATCH IT AGAIN?

YES
ONLY IF THERE IS POPCORN
NO

RECOMMEND IT?

YES
UMMMM.....
NO

FAVORITE CHARACTER *and* WHY?

FAVORITE QUOTE OR LINE

MOVIE GENRE

FAMILY FAVORITE?
YES ? NO

WHO SELECTED IT?

WHO IS WATCHING?

MOVIE NAME

TODAY IS:

RATING

★ ★ ★ ★ ★

STARRING

What did you like or dislike about the movie?

What did you learn from the movie?

WATCH IT AGAIN?

RECOMMEND IT?

FAVORITE CHARACTER and WHY?

MOVIE GENRE

FAMILY FAVORITE?
YES ? NO

WHO SELECTED IT?

WHO IS WATCHING?

FAVORITE QUOTE OR LINE

MOVIE NAME

TODAY IS:

RATING

★ ★ ★ ★ ★

STARRING

What did you like or dislike about the movie?

What did you learn from the movie?

WATCH IT AGAIN?

YES
ONLY IF THERE IS POPCORN
NO

RECOMMEND IT?

YES
UMMMM.....
NO

FAVORITE CHARACTER and WHY?

MOVIE GENRE

FAMILY FAVORITE?
YES ? NO

WHO SELECTED IT?

WHO IS WATCHING?

FAVORITE QUOTE OR LINE

MOVIE NAME

TODAY IS:

RATING

STARRING

What did you like or dislike about the movie?

What did you learn from the movie?

FAVORITE CHARACTER and WHY?

MOVIE GENRE

FAMILY FAVORITE?

YES ? NO

WHO SELECTED IT?

WHO IS WATCHING?

FAVORITE QUOTE OR LINE

WATCH IT AGAIN?

YES
ONLY IF THERE IS POPCORN
NO

RECOMMEND IT?

YES
UMMMM.....
NO

MOVIE NAME

TODAY IS:

RATING

★ ★ ★ ★ ★

STARRING

What did you like or dislike about the movie?

What did you learn from the movie?

FAVORITE CHARACTER and WHY?

FAVORITE QUOTE OR LINE

MOVIE GENRE

FAMILY FAVORITE?
YES ? NO

WHO SELECTED IT?

WHO IS WATCHING?

WATCH IT AGAIN?

YES
ONLY IF THERE IS POPCORN
NO

RECOMMEND IT?

YES
UMMMM.....
NO

MOVIE NAME

TODAY IS:

RATING

STARRING

What did you like or dislike about the movie?

What did you learn from the movie?

WATCH IT AGAIN?

YES
ONLY IF THERE IS POPCORN
NO

RECOMMEND IT?

YES
UMMMM.....
NO

FAVORITE CHARACTER and WHY?

FAVORITE QUOTE OR LINE

MOVIE GENRE

FAMILY FAVORITE?

YES ? NO

WHO SELECTED IT?

WHO IS WATCHING?

MOVIE NAME

TODAY IS:

RATING

★ ★ ★ ★ ★

STARRING

What did you like or dislike about the movie?

What did you learn from the movie?

WATCH IT AGAIN?

YES
ONLY IF THERE IS POPCORN
NO

RECOMMEND IT?

YES
UMMMM.....
NO

FAVORITE CHARACTER *and* WHY?

FAVORITE QUOTE OR LINE

MOVIE GENRE

FAMILY FAVORITE?
YES ? NO

WHO SELECTED IT?

WHO IS WATCHING?

MOVIE NAME

TODAY IS:

RATING

☆ ☆ ☆ ☆ ☆

STARRING

What did you like or dislike about the movie?

What did you learn from the movie?

FAVORITE CHARACTER and WHY?

MOVIE GENRE

FAMILY FAVORITE?
YES ? NO

WHO SELECTED IT?

WHO IS WATCHING?

FAVORITE QUOTE OR LINE

WATCH IT AGAIN?

YES
ONLY IF THERE IS POPCORN
NO

RECOMMEND IT?

YES
UMMMM.....
NO

MOVIE NAME

TODAY IS:

RATING

★ ★ ★ ★ ★

STARRING

What did you like or dislike

about the movie?

What did you learn

from the movie?

FAVORITE CHARACTER
and WHY?

MOVIE GENRE

FAMILY FAVORITE?

YES ? NO

WHO SELECTED IT?

WHO IS WATCHING?

FAVORITE QUOTE OR LINE

WATCH IT AGAIN?

YES
ONLY IF THERE
IS POPCORN
NO

RECOMMEND IT?

YES
UMMMM.....
NO

MOVIE NAME

TODAY IS:

RATING

★ ★ ★ ★ ★

STARRING

What did you like or dislike about the movie?

What did you learn from the movie?

WATCH IT AGAIN?

YES
ONLY IF THERE IS POPCORN
NO

RECOMMEND IT?

YES
UMMMM.....
NO

FAVORITE CHARACTER and WHY?

FAVORITE QUOTE OR LINE

MOVIE GENRE

FAMILY FAVORITE?

YES ? NO

WHO SELECTED IT?

WHO IS WATCHING?

MOVIE NAME

TODAY IS:

RATING

⭐ ⭐ ⭐ ⭐ ⭐

STARRING

What did you like or dislike about the movie?

What did you learn from the movie?

FAVORITE CHARACTER and WHY?

MOVIE GENRE

FAMILY FAVORITE?
YES ? NO

WHO SELECTED IT?

WHO IS WATCHING?

FAVORITE QUOTE OR LINE

WATCH IT AGAIN?

YES
ONLY IF THERE IS POPCORN
NO

RECOMMEND IT?

YES
UMMMM.....
NO

MOVIE NAME

TODAY IS:

RATING

STARRING

What did you like or dislike about the movie?

What did you learn from the movie?

FAVORITE CHARACTER and WHY?

MOVIE GENRE

FAMILY FAVORITE?
YES ? NO

WHO SELECTED IT?

WHO IS WATCHING?

FAVORITE QUOTE OR LINE

WATCH IT AGAIN?

YES
ONLY IF THERE IS POPCORN
NO

RECOMMEND IT?

YES
UMMMM.....
NO

MOVIE NAME

TODAY IS:

RATING

★ ★ ★ ★ ★

STARRING

What did you like or dislike about the movie?

What did you learn from the movie?

WATCH IT AGAIN?

YES
ONLY IF THERE IS POPCORN
NO

RECOMMEND IT?

YES
UMMMM......
NO

FAVORITE CHARACTER and WHY?

FAVORITE QUOTE OR LINE

MOVIE GENRE

FAMILY FAVORITE?
YES ? NO

WHO SELECTED IT?

WHO IS WATCHING?

MOVIE NAME

TODAY IS:

RATING

★ ★ ★ ★ ★

STARRING

What did you like or dislike about the movie?

What did you learn from the movie?

WATCH IT AGAIN?

YES
ONLY IF THERE IS POPCORN
NO

RECOMMEND IT?

YES
UMMMM.....
NO

FAVORITE CHARACTER and WHY?

FAVORITE QUOTE OR LINE

MOVIE GENRE

FAMILY FAVORITE?
YES ? NO

WHO SELECTED IT?

WHO IS WATCHING?

MOVIE NAME

TODAY IS:

RATING

★★★★★

STARRING

What did you like or dislike about the movie?

What did you learn from the movie?

FAVORITE CHARACTER *and* WHY?

MOVIE GENRE

FAMILY FAVORITE?
YES ? NO

WHO SELECTED IT?

WHO IS WATCHING?

FAVORITE QUOTE OR LINE

WATCH IT AGAIN?

YES
ONLY IF THERE IS POPCORN
NO

RECOMMEND IT?

YES
UMMMM.....
NO

MOVIE NAME

TODAY IS:

RATING

STARRING

What did you like or dislike about the movie?

What did you learn from the movie?

FAVORITE CHARACTER and WHY?

MOVIE GENRE

FAMILY FAVORITE?
YES ? NO

WHO SELECTED IT?

WHO IS WATCHING?

FAVORITE QUOTE OR LINE

WATCH IT AGAIN?

YES
ONLY IF THERE IS POPCORN
NO

RECOMMEND IT?

YES
UMMMM.....
NO

MOVIE NAME

TODAY IS:

RATING

STARRING

What did you like or dislike about the movie?

FAVORITE CHARACTER and, WHY?

MOVIE GENRE

FAMILY FAVORITE?
YES ? NO

WHO SELECTED IT?

What did you learn from the movie?

WHO IS WATCHING?

FAVORITE QUOTE OR LINE

WATCH IT AGAIN?

YES
ONLY IF THERE IS POPCORN
NO

RECOMMEND IT?

YES
UMMMM.....
NO

MOVIE NAME

TODAY IS:

RATING
★ ★ ★ ★ ★

STARRING

What did you like or dislike about the movie?

What did you learn from the movie?

WATCH IT AGAIN?

YES
ONLY IF THERE IS POPCORN
NO

RECOMMEND IT?

YES
UMMMM.....
NO

FAVORITE CHARACTER and WHY?

FAVORITE QUOTE OR LINE

MOVIE GENRE

FAMILY FAVORITE?
YES ? NO

WHO SELECTED IT?

WHO IS WATCHING?

MOVIE NAME

TODAY IS:

RATING

STARRING

What did you like or dislike about the movie?

FAVORITE CHARACTER *and* WHY?

MOVIE GENRE

FAMILY FAVORITE?

YES ? NO

WHO SELECTED IT?

What did you learn from the movie?

WHO IS WATCHING?

FAVORITE QUOTE OR LINE

WATCH IT AGAIN?

YES
ONLY IF THERE IS POPCORN
NO

RECOMMEND IT?

YES
UMMMM.....
NO

MOVIE NAME

TODAY IS:

RATING

STARRING

What did you like or dislike about the movie?

What did you learn from the movie?

FAVORITE CHARACTER
and WHY?

MOVIE GENRE

FAMILY FAVORITE?

YES ? NO

WHO SELECTED IT?

WHO IS WATCHING?

FAVORITE QUOTE OR LINE

WATCH IT AGAIN?

YES
ONLY IF THERE IS POPCORN
NO

RECOMMEND IT?

YES
UMMMM.....
NO

MOVIE NAME

TODAY IS:

RATING

★ ★ ★ ★ ★

STARRING

What did you like or dislike about the movie?

What did you learn from the movie?

WATCH IT AGAIN?

YES

ONLY IF THERE IS POPCORN

NO

RECOMMEND IT?

YES

UMMMM.....

NO

FAVORITE CHARACTER
and WHY?

FAVORITE QUOTE OR LINE

MOVIE GENRE

FAMILY FAVORITE?
YES ? NO

WHO SELECTED IT?

WHO IS WATCHING?

MOVIE NAME

TODAY IS:

RATING

★ ★ ★ ★ ★

STARRING

What did you like or dislike about the movie?

What did you learn from the movie?

FAVORITE CHARACTER and WHY?

FAVORITE QUOTE OR LINE

MOVIE GENRE

FAMILY FAVORITE?
YES ? NO

WHO SELECTED IT?

WHO IS WATCHING?

WATCH IT AGAIN?

YES
ONLY IF THERE
IS POPCORN
NO

RECOMMEND IT?

YES
UMMMM.....
NO

MOVIE NAME

TODAY IS:

RATING

★ ★ ★ ★ ★

STARRING

What did you like or dislike about the movie?

What did you learn from the movie?

FAVORITE CHARACTER and WHY?

MOVIE GENRE

FAMILY FAVORITE?
YES ? NO

WHO SELECTED IT?

WHO IS WATCHING?

FAVORITE QUOTE OR LINE

WATCH IT AGAIN?

YES
ONLY IF THERE IS POPCORN
NO

RECOMMEND IT?

YES
UMMMM.....
NO

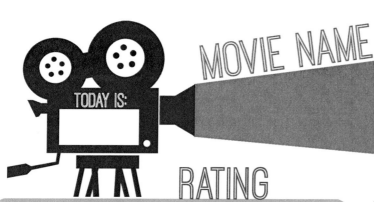

MOVIE NAME

TODAY IS:

RATING

★ ★ ★ ★ ★

STARRING

What did you like or dislike about the movie?

What did you learn from the movie?

FAVORITE CHARACTER and WHY?

MOVIE GENRE

FAMILY FAVORITE?

YES ? NO

WHO SELECTED IT?

WHO IS WATCHING?

FAVORITE QUOTE OR LINE

WATCH IT AGAIN?

YES
ONLY IF THERE IS POPCORN
NO

RECOMMEND IT?

YES
UMMMM.....
NO

MOVIE NAME

TODAY IS:

RATING

☆☆☆☆☆

STARRING

What did you like or dislike about the movie?

What did you learn from the movie?

FAVORITE CHARACTER
and WHY?

MOVIE GENRE

FAMILY FAVORITE?
YES ? NO

WHO SELECTED IT?

WHO IS WATCHING?

FAVORITE QUOTE OR LINE

WATCH IT AGAIN?

YES
ONLY IF THERE
IS POPCORN
NO

RECOMMEND IT?

YES
UMMMM.....
NO

MOVIE NAME

TODAY IS:

RATING

☆ ☆ ☆ ☆ ☆

STARRING

What did you like or dislike about the movie?

What did you learn from the movie?

FAVORITE CHARACTER and WHY?

FAVORITE QUOTE OR LINE

MOVIE GENRE

FAMILY FAVORITE?

YES ? NO

WHO SELECTED IT?

WHO IS WATCHING?

WATCH IT AGAIN?

YES
ONLY IF THERE
IS POPCORN
NO

RECOMMEND IT?

YES
UMMMM.....
NO

MOVIE NAME

TODAY IS:

RATING

★ ★ ★ ★ ★

STARRING

What did you like or dislike about the movie?

What did you learn from the movie?

WATCH IT AGAIN?

YES
ONLY IF THERE IS POPCORN
NO

RECOMMEND IT?

YES
UMMMM.....
NO

FAVORITE CHARACTER and WHY?

FAVORITE QUOTE OR LINE

MOVIE GENRE

FAMILY FAVORITE?
YES ? NO

WHO SELECTED IT?

WHO IS WATCHING?

MOVIE NAME

TODAY IS:

RATING

STARRING

What did you like or dislike

about the movie?

from the movie?

What did you learn

FAVORITE CHARACTER
and WHY?

FAVORITE QUOTE OR LINE

MOVIE GENRE

FAMILY FAVORITE?

YES ? NO

WHO SELECTED IT?

WHO IS WATCHING?

WATCH IT AGAIN?

YES

ONLY IF THERE
IS POPCORN

NO

RECOMMEND IT?

YES

UMMMM.....

NO

MOVIE NAME

TODAY IS:

RATING

STARRING

What did you like or dislike about the movie?

What did you learn from the movie?

WATCH IT AGAIN?

YES
ONLY IF THERE IS POPCORN
NO

RECOMMEND IT?

YES
UMMMM.....
NO

FAVORITE CHARACTER *and* WHY?

MOVIE GENRE

FAMILY FAVORITE?
YES ? NO

WHO SELECTED IT?

WHO IS WATCHING?

FAVORITE QUOTE OR LINE

MOVIE NAME

TODAY IS:

RATING

STARRING

What did you like or dislike about the movie?

FAVORITE CHARACTER and WHY?

MOVIE GENRE

FAMILY FAVORITE?

YES ? NO

WHO SELECTED IT?

What did you learn from the movie?

WHO IS WATCHING?

FAVORITE QUOTE OR LINE

WATCH IT AGAIN?

YES
ONLY IF THERE IS POPCORN
NO

RECOMMEND IT?

YES
UMMMM.....
NO

MOVIE NAME

TODAY IS:

RATING

★ ★ ★ ★ ★

STARRING

What did you like or dislike about the movie?

What did you learn from the movie?

WATCH IT AGAIN?

YES
ONLY IF THERE IS POPCORN
NO

RECOMMEND IT?

YES
UMMMM.....
NO

FAVORITE CHARACTER and WHY?

MOVIE GENRE

FAMILY FAVORITE?
YES ? NO

WHO SELECTED IT?

WHO IS WATCHING?

FAVORITE QUOTE OR LINE

MOVIE NAME

TODAY IS:

RATING

STARRING

What did you like or dislike

about the movie?

What did you learn

from the movie?

FAVORITE CHARACTER and WHY?

FAVORITE QUOTE OR LINE

MOVIE GENRE

FAMILY FAVORITE?
YES ? NO

WHO SELECTED IT?

WHO IS WATCHING?

WATCH IT AGAIN?

YES
ONLY IF THERE IS POPCORN
NO

RECOMMEND IT?

YES
UMMMM.....
NO

MOVIE NAME

TODAY IS:

RATING

STARRING

What did you like or dislike about the movie?

What did you learn from the movie?

FAVORITE CHARACTER *and* WHY?

MOVIE GENRE

FAMILY FAVORITE?
YES ? NO

WHO SELECTED IT?

WHO IS WATCHING?

FAVORITE QUOTE OR LINE

WATCH IT AGAIN?

YES
ONLY IF THERE IS POPCORN
NO

RECOMMEND IT?

YES
UMMMM.....
NO

MOVIE NAME

TODAY IS:

RATING

☆ ☆ ☆ ☆ ☆

STARRING

What did you like or dislike about the movie?

What did you learn from the movie?

WATCH IT AGAIN?

RECOMMEND IT?

FAVORITE CHARACTER *and* WHY?

FAVORITE QUOTE OR LINE

MOVIE GENRE

FAMILY FAVORITE?

YES ? NO

WHO SELECTED IT?

WHO IS WATCHING?

MOVIE NAME

TODAY IS:

RATING

STARRING

What did you like or dislike about the movie?

FAVORITE CHARACTER and WHY?

MOVIE GENRE

FAMILY FAVORITE?
YES ? NO

WHO SELECTED IT?

What did you learn from the movie?

WHO IS WATCHING?

FAVORITE QUOTE OR LINE

WATCH IT AGAIN?

RECOMMEND IT?

YES
ONLY IF THERE IS POPCORN
NO

YES
UMMMM.....
NO

MOVIE NAME

TODAY IS:

RATING

⭐ ⭐ ⭐ ⭐ ⭐

STARRING

What did you like or dislike about the movie?

What did you learn from the movie?

FAVORITE CHARACTER and WHY?

MOVIE GENRE

FAMILY FAVORITE?
YES   ?   NO

WHO SELECTED IT?

WHO IS WATCHING?

FAVORITE QUOTE OR LINE

WATCH IT AGAIN?

YES
ONLY IF THERE IS POPCORN
NO

RECOMMEND IT?

YES
UMMMM.....
NO

MOVIE NAME

TODAY IS:

RATING

STARRING

What did you like or dislike about the movie?

What did you learn from the movie?

FAVORITE CHARACTER and WHY?

MOVIE GENRE

FAMILY FAVORITE?
YES ? NO

WHO SELECTED IT?

WHO IS WATCHING?

FAVORITE QUOTE OR LINE

WATCH IT AGAIN?
YES
ONLY IF THERE IS POPCORN
NO

RECOMMEND IT?
YES
UMMMM.....
NO

MOVIE NAME

TODAY IS:

RATING

STARRING

What did you like or dislike about the movie?

What did you learn from the movie?

FAVORITE CHARACTER and WHY?

MOVIE GENRE

FAMILY FAVORITE?
YES ? NO

WHO SELECTED IT?

WHO IS WATCHING?

FAVORITE QUOTE OR LINE

WATCH IT AGAIN?

YES
ONLY IF THERE IS POPCORN
NO

RECOMMEND IT?

YES
UMMMM.....
NO

MOVIE NAME

TODAY IS:

RATING

STARRING

What did you like or dislike about the movie?

What did you learn from the movie?

FAVORITE CHARACTER *and* WHY?

MOVIE GENRE

FAMILY FAVORITE?
YES ? NO

WHO SELECTED IT?

WHO IS WATCHING?

FAVORITE QUOTE OR LINE

WATCH IT AGAIN?

YES
ONLY IF THERE IS POPCORN
NO

RECOMMEND IT?

YES
UMMMM.....
NO

MOVIE NAME

TODAY IS:

RATING

STARRING

What did you like or dislike

about the movie?

What did you learn

from the movie?

FAVORITE CHARACTER and WHY?

MOVIE GENRE

FAMILY FAVORITE?
YES ? NO

WHO SELECTED IT?

WHO IS WATCHING?

FAVORITE QUOTE OR LINE

WATCH IT AGAIN?

YES
ONLY IF THERE IS POPCORN
NO

RECOMMEND IT?

YES
UMMMM.....
NO

MOVIE NAME

TODAY IS:

RATING

STARRING

What did you like or dislike
about the movie?

What did you learn
from the movie?

WATCH IT AGAIN?

YES

ONLY IF THERE
IS POPCORN

NO

RECOMMEND IT?

YES

UMMMM.....

NO

FAVORITE CHARACTER
and WHY?

FAVORITE QUOTE OR LINE

MOVIE GENRE

FAMILY FAVORITE?

YES ? NO

WHO SELECTED IT?

WHO IS WATCHING?

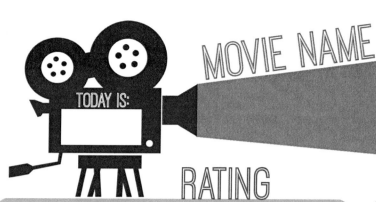

MOVIE NAME

TODAY IS:

RATING

⭐ ⭐ ⭐ ⭐ ⭐

STARRING

What did you like or dislike about the movie?

What did you learn from the movie?

FAVORITE CHARACTER and WHY?

MOVIE GENRE

FAMILY FAVORITE?
YES ? NO

WHO SELECTED IT?

WHO IS WATCHING?

FAVORITE QUOTE OR LINE

WATCH IT AGAIN?

YES
ONLY IF THERE IS POPCORN
NO

RECOMMEND IT?

YES
UMMMM.....
NO

MOVIE NAME

TODAY IS:

RATING

★ ★ ★ ★ ★

STARRING

What did you like or dislike about the movie?

What did you learn from the movie?

FAVORITE CHARACTER *and,* WHY?

FAVORITE QUOTE OR LINE

MOVIE GENRE

FAMILY FAVORITE?
YES ? NO

WHO SELECTED IT?

WHO IS WATCHING?

WATCH IT AGAIN?

YES

ONLY IF THERE IS POPCORN

NO

RECOMMEND IT?

YES

UMMMM.....

NO

MOVIE NAME

TODAY IS:

RATING

☆ ☆ ☆ ☆ ☆

STARRING

What did you like or dislike about the movie?

What did you learn from the movie?

FAVORITE CHARACTER and WHY?

MOVIE GENRE

FAMILY FAVORITE?
YES ? NO

WHO SELECTED IT?

WHO IS WATCHING?

FAVORITE QUOTE OR LINE

WATCH IT AGAIN?
YES
ONLY IF THERE IS POPCORN
NO

RECOMMEND IT?
YES
UMMMM.....
NO

MOVIE NAME

TODAY IS:

RATING

STARRING

What did you like or dislike about the movie?

What did you learn from the movie?

FAVORITE CHARACTER
and WHY?

MOVIE GENRE

FAMILY FAVORITE?
YES ? NO

WHO SELECTED IT?

WHO IS WATCHING?

FAVORITE QUOTE OR LINE

WATCH IT AGAIN?

YES
ONLY IF THERE
IS POPCORN
NO

RECOMMEND IT?

YES
UMMMM.....
NO

MOVIE NAME

TODAY IS:

RATING

STARRING

What did you like or dislike about the movie?

What did you learn from the movie?

WATCH IT AGAIN?

YES
ONLY IF THERE IS POPCORN
NO

RECOMMEND IT?

YES
UMMMM.....
NO

FAVORITE CHARACTER and WHY?

FAVORITE QUOTE OR LINE

MOVIE GENRE

FAMILY FAVORITE?

YES ? NO

WHO SELECTED IT?

WHO IS WATCHING?

MOVIE NAME

TODAY IS:

RATING

★ ★ ★ ★ ★

STARRING

What did you like or dislike about the movie?

What did you learn from the movie?

WATCH IT AGAIN?

YES
ONLY IF THERE IS POPCORN
NO

RECOMMEND IT?

YES
UMMMM.....
NO

FAVORITE CHARACTER
and WHY?

FAVORITE QUOTE OR LINE

MOVIE GENRE

FAMILY FAVORITE?
YES ? NO

WHO SELECTED IT?

WHO IS WATCHING?

MOVIE NAME

TODAY IS:

RATING

STARRING

What did you like or dislike about the movie?

What did you learn from the movie?

FAVORITE CHARACTER and, WHY?

MOVIE GENRE

FAMILY FAVORITE?
YES ? NO

WHO SELECTED IT?

WHO IS WATCHING?

FAVORITE QUOTE OR LINE

WATCH IT AGAIN?

YES
ONLY IF THERE IS POPCORN
NO

RECOMMEND IT?

YES
UMMMM.....
NO

MOVIE NAME

TODAY IS:

RATING

★ ★ ★ ★ ★

STARRING

What did you like or dislike about the movie?

What did you learn from the movie?

WATCH IT AGAIN?

YES
ONLY IF THERE IS POPCORN
NO

RECOMMEND IT?

YES
UMMMM.....
NO

FAVORITE CHARACTER and, WHY?

MOVIE GENRE

FAMILY FAVORITE?
YES ? NO

WHO SELECTED IT?

WHO IS WATCHING?

FAVORITE QUOTE OR LINE

MOVIE NAME

TODAY IS:

RATING

STARRING

What did you like or dislike about the movie?

What did you learn from the movie?

FAVORITE CHARACTER and WHY?

MOVIE GENRE

FAMILY FAVORITE?
YES ? NO

WHO SELECTED IT?

WHO IS WATCHING?

FAVORITE QUOTE OR LINE

WATCH IT AGAIN?

YES
ONLY IF THERE IS POPCORN
NO

RECOMMEND IT?

YES
UMMMM.....
NO

MOVIE NAME

TODAY IS:

RATING

★ ★ ★ ★ ★

STARRING

What did you like or dislike about the movie?

What did you learn from the movie?

WATCH IT AGAIN?

YES
ONLY IF THERE IS POPCORN
NO

RECOMMEND IT?

YES
UMMMM.....
NO

FAVORITE CHARACTER and WHY?

MOVIE GENRE

FAMILY FAVORITE?
YES ? NO

WHO SELECTED IT?

WHO IS WATCHING?

FAVORITE QUOTE OR LINE

MOVIE NAME

TODAY IS:

RATING

☆ ☆ ☆ ☆ ☆

STARRING

What did you like or dislike
about the movie?

What did you learn
from the movie?

WATCH IT AGAIN?

YES

ONLY IF THERE IS POPCORN

NO

RECOMMEND IT?

YES

UMMMM.....

NO

FAVORITE CHARACTER and WHY?

MOVIE GENRE

FAMILY FAVORITE?

YES ? NO

WHO SELECTED IT?

WHO IS WATCHING?

FAVORITE QUOTE OR LINE

MOVIE NAME

TODAY IS:

RATING

STARRING

What did you like or dislike about the movie?

What did you learn from the movie?

FAVORITE CHARACTER and WHY?

MOVIE GENRE

FAMILY FAVORITE?
YES ? NO

WHO SELECTED IT?

WHO IS WATCHING?

FAVORITE QUOTE OR LINE

WATCH IT AGAIN?
YES
ONLY IF THERE IS POPCORN
NO

RECOMMEND IT?
YES
UMMMM.....
NO

MOVIE NAME

TODAY IS:

RATING

STARRING

What did you like or dislike

about the movie?

What did you learn from the movie?

FAVORITE CHARACTER and WHY?

MOVIE GENRE

FAMILY FAVORITE?

YES ? NO

WHO SELECTED IT?

WHO IS WATCHING?

FAVORITE QUOTE OR LINE

WATCH IT AGAIN?

YES

ONLY IF THERE IS POPCORN

NO

RECOMMEND IT?

YES

UMMMM.....

NO

MOVIE NAME

TODAY IS:

RATING

STARRING

What did you like or dislike about the movie?

What did you learn from the movie?

FAVORITE CHARACTER *and* WHY?

MOVIE GENRE

FAMILY FAVORITE?
YES ? NO

WHO SELECTED IT?

WHO IS WATCHING?

FAVORITE QUOTE OR LINE

WATCH IT AGAIN?

YES
ONLY IF THERE IS POPCORN
NO

RECOMMEND IT?

YES
UMMMM.....
NO

MOVIE NAME

TODAY IS:

RATING

☆ ☆ ☆ ☆ ☆

STARRING

What did you like or dislike about the movie?

What did you learn from the movie?

WATCH IT AGAIN?

YES
ONLY IF THERE IS POPCORN
NO

RECOMMEND IT?

YES
UMMMM.....
NO

FAVORITE CHARACTER and WHY?

FAVORITE QUOTE OR LINE

MOVIE GENRE

FAMILY FAVORITE?
YES ? NO

WHO SELECTED IT?

WHO IS WATCHING?

MOVIE NAME

TODAY IS:

RATING

STARRING

What did you like or dislike

about the movie?

What did you learn

from the movie?

FAVORITE CHARACTER
and WHY?

FAVORITE QUOTE OR LINE

MOVIE GENRE

FAMILY FAVORITE?
YES ? NO

WHO SELECTED IT?

WHO IS WATCHING?

WATCH IT AGAIN?

YES
ONLY IF THERE
IS POPCORN
NO

RECOMMEND IT?

YES
UMMMM.....
NO

MOVIE NAME

TODAY IS:

RATING

STARRING

What did you like or dislike about the movie?

What did you learn from the movie?

FAVORITE CHARACTER and WHY?

MOVIE GENRE

FAMILY FAVORITE?
YES   ?   NO

WHO SELECTED IT?

WHO IS WATCHING?

FAVORITE QUOTE OR LINE

WATCH IT AGAIN?

YES
ONLY IF THERE IS POPCORN
NO

RECOMMEND IT?

YES
UMMMM.....
NO

Family FAVORITES

ACKNOWLEDGEMENTS

I'd like to thank the following people for their kind and generous support on my journey of creating Family Movie Journal.

To my team:

To Cynthia Morris, from Original Impulse, who was a fantastic coach throughout this fun process. I appreciate you showing me the way. Your guidance, support and friendship are deeply appreciated.

To Bonnie Steves from BJS & Associates for your inspiration and design direction.

To Jennifer Burrell from Fresh Vision Design for your creative designs and inspiration. You brought to life what was in my heart and soul. I can't thank you enough.

To Kim Sabbag, for managing all the moving parts so well.

I could not have created Family Movie Journal without each of you.

To my husband and kids for their sweet inspiration along the way. You make every Sunday movie night fun and I love what this has brought to our family. You are at the heart of this special project.

To My dear friends, you know who you are, for your support and enthusiasm as Family Movie Journal came to life.

I'd like to thank my mother, Sandy, for this creative bug I have inside. I know I got this inspiration from you mom and I love that it's passing through our family. Caylee is next and I can see it in her already. Love you.

Lastly, I'd like to say thanks to this glorious universe for reminding me that you can really do anything you want in life if you set your mind to it.....and have a lot of fun along the way.

ENJOY!

Let's STAY CONNECTED

Follow us on Facebook FAMILY MOVIE JOURNAL
Tell us about that movie that changed the way your family connected. Share how using the Family Movie Journal contributed to a richer family experience.

Post your family pictures on Instagram and Facebook - have some fun with this! We learn so much by sharing our treasured experiences with each other.

Be sure to use our hashtag #FamilyMovieJournal.

On Fun Family Fridays on Facebook you can post your favorite movies and movies that are on your "must see" list. We hope you'll enjoy sharing your favorites and getting recommendations from other families around the globe.

You'll love what we are cooking up to create even more fun and connection. Be the first to hear about it by joining our mailing list. http://bit.ly/familymoviejournal

To connect with me directly, write to me at: laurie@familymoviejournal.com

I can't wait to see how you use your Family Movie Journal! Cheers to growing and deepening our connection.

75589760R00084

Made in the USA
San Bernardino, CA
04 May 2018